*Passing Through Customs*

# Passing Through Customs

## new and selected poems

### GIBBONS RUARK

Louisiana State University Press
*Baton Rouge* 1999

Designer: Michele Myatt Quinn
Typeface: Sabon
Typesetter: Coghill Composition
Printer and binder: Edwards Brothers, Inc.

Library of Congress Cataloging-in-Publication Data

Ruark, Gibbons.
    Passing through customs : new and selected poems / Gibbons Ruark.
        p.   cm.
    ISBN 0-8071-2361-7 (cloth : alk. paper)—
    ISBN 0-8071-2362-5 (pbk: alk. paper)
        I. Title.
    PS3568.U17P37   1999
    811'.54—dc21                                                    98-44083
                                                                         CIP

Many of the poems herein have been selected from previous collections of poetry by the author: *A Program for Survival* (University Press of Virginia, 1971), copyright © 1971 by the Rector and Visitors of the University of Virginia; *Reeds* (Texas Tech University Press, 1978), copyright © 1978 by Texas Tech University; *Keeping Company* (The Johns Hopkins University Press, 1983), copyright © 1983 by The Johns Hopkins University Press; and *Rescue the Perishing* (Louisiana State University Press, 1991), copyright © 1980, 1983, 1984, 1985, 1986, 1987, 1988, 1989, 1990, 1991 by Gibbons Ruark.
    The poems herein that appeared in *Keeping Company* (The Johns Hopkins University Press, 1983) are reprinted with permission of The Johns Hopkins University Press.
    Grateful acknowledgment is also made to the editors of the following publications, in which the poems noted first appeared: "Autumn Elegy" in *Willow Springs;* "Blue Shades for a Daughter," "Elegiac Anyway," "Househusbandry," "A Road Map for Reviewers," and "This Table" in *Shenandoah;* "Hybrid Magnolias in Late April" and "Late December" in *The New Republic;* "On Hearing My Father's Voice in a Dead Sleep" in *American Poetry Review;* "Robert Frost to Ezra Pound's Daughter from His Deathbed" in *Hampden-Sydney Poetry Review;* and "Two Anglo-Irish Sonnets" in *The Midwest Quarterly.*
    "Swamp Mallows" originally appeared in *The Store of Joys: Writers Celebrate the North Carolina Museum of Art's Fiftieth Anniversary,* ed. Huston Paschal (North Carolina Museum of Art in association with John F. Blair, Publisher, 1997).
    "A Vacant Lot" also appeared in *The Pushcart Prize, XV: Best of the Small Presses* (Wainscott, N.Y.: Pushcart Press, 1990). "Househusbandry" was featured in the on-line anthology *Poetry Daily* in July 1997, and "Elegiac Anyway" in July 1998.
    The author extends his grateful thanks to the National Endowment for the Arts for fellowships that supported work on many of these poems, and to Bernard and Mary Loughlin of the Tyrone Guthrie Centre in Ireland.

This publication is supported in part by a grant from the National Endowment for the Arts.

*for Gabriel and Sarah and Tian*

# Contents

*Passing Through Customs*

## Words for Unaccompanied Voice at Dunmore Head

One old friend who never writes me tells another:
The boy has need of lyrical friends around him.
Don't ask me how I ever found that out,

Given as I am to these fugitive headlands
Where not so long ago the news from Dublin
Arrived washed up with driftwood from the States,

Where the gulls rehearse the local word for weather
And then free-fall through ragged clouds to the sea wrack.
The bar at the end of the world is three miles east.

Last night the music there ascended with the smoke
From a turf fire and showered down in dying sparks
That fell on lovers and the lonely ones alike

Where they cycled the dark roads home or lingered
By a bridge till every cottage light was out—
Fell silent from the night as innocent as milkweed.

All night those soft stars burned in my watchful sleep.
At dawn I abandoned my rackety faithless car
To its own persuasions, took up a stick

And leaned uphill into the wind for the summit.
No music here but the raw alarms of seabirds
And the tireless water high against the cliff face.

No more the flute and the whiskeyed tenor rising,
The chorus of faces in the drift of smoke.
This is the rock where solitude scrapes its keel

And listens into the light for an echo.
This has to be good practice for that last
Cold wave of emptiness on whatever shore,

But why do the reckoners in my nightmares
Never ask me what I said to the speechless
Assembly of whitecaps instead of was

There anyone arm-in-arm with me as I spoke?

# Night Fishing

We have come again, my father and I,
To the edge of the known land, to the streak
Of sand that lips the undermining sea.
But we are not allowed this time to speak

Of horizons, for the sun has dropped
Behind us, and night is all of a piece.
The lights go out in the cottages propped
Above the black dunes, room by room the lights

Go out, the children fall asleep, and soon
Whole families sleep as calm as children,
Nursed by the motions of the wind and tide.
My fishing rod springs and quivers and the line

Loops over the breakers; I watch the sinker
Splash and start to reel in steadily, steadily,
Feeling the current drag. Downshore, my father
Tosses with a pitcher's ease, then braces

His legs against the undertow and waits.
His cigarette stings a hole in the dark.
The odor of fish grows stronger as the wind
Switches and the sea crawls to us with its sharks.

My father stands like a driven piling.
I move downshore. Somewhere not far inland,
Where the afternoon's shrimpboats are nuzzling
In their sleep, his hometown leans into the river.

Below us, empty of fishers, the old pier
Sways over climbing waters, the salt wash
Rinses the pilings scabbed with barnacles.
The timbers shudder in the tidal rush.

The water lifts, but we do not move back
Until the seaweed swirls about our thighs
And empty bait trays tumble in the slack.
We reel and pull and reel and pull again.

Somewhere in that darkened row of houses
Our women sleep in their beautiful order,
But here on the swift-dissolving shore
I drift to my father in the night's one water.

Yearly we come to this familiar coast
To wade beside each other in the shallows,
Reaching for bluefish in the ocean's darkness
Till our lines are tangled and our tackle lost.

# Leaving Hatteras

Deep summer is time forgetful of its calling,
The place a screened porch hugging the home Atlantic,
My brother's voice beside me: All you do is close
Your eyes. The surf's invisible below the dunes,
But its sound is the fallback and lift of memory.

After the days of heat and stillness, heat piling
Over our heads in columns ranked immovable,
The storm-cooled breezes riffle every window shade,
Freshness billows and flaps the air like a sail.
All I do is close my eyes. A screen door shudders
And bangs and a boy lights out for the water

And it is south of here by thirty years and more
Where the shore curls inward and the dunes are lower
And a boy can see his father from the water
Cleaning and oiling his tackle in a porch chair.
By the time he gets it right the fish will vanish.

One afternoon he walks as far as the shell line
Marking the tide's reach, remembers his scaling knife,
And goes back in and puts his feet up for a minute
And wakes to a plate of oysters on the table.
Now on a sleeping-porch just wavering toward its name
My brother and I are pulling on our road clothes

Halfheartedly, a sleeve or a sock at a time,
As if we were young and moving house all over
And not just going home at the end of summer.
There is a snapshot of a kindred moment somewhere,
More formal, though we stand there in our undershorts,

August in Carolina laving our faces,
The sun through stained glass dim but unrelenting.
It is the choir room before my sister's wedding,
My father reaching to help us with our cuff links,
His brow lit with sweat or the new forgetfulness.
Here what looks like water shivers over the screens

And we breathe deep, two of us only, buttoning
Our sleeves and zipping up the nylon duffel bags,
Unless you count the lazybones in the doorway,
Stretching himself and rubbing his eyes with his knuckles,
Blinking like a child as the room turns familiar.

# Transatlantic Summer Elegy

Dusk in Kinvara. An old man quietly sings
To the air. In a distant time zone, late summer
Is leaving town. From houses with small children,
The yellow porch lights flick on after supper,
Hazy constellations of dim low stars.
High stars are still, the air so still the odor
Of honeysuckle sleeps in the hedges.
This is a night to keep still in the branches
Till someone on a porch starts calling you home.
Each house circled by light is holding its breath
When suddenly out of nowhere a breeze rises
And the whole of the great night tree starts swaying
As if it were not all the leaves but one.
The wrong old man keeps singing in Kinvara.

## Polio

The snore of midsummer flies at the screen,
Afternoon's tepid fog crawling my sleep.
In my unrelenting dream the fire truck
Peals round the corner, and when I wake
The sirens still confound me. From the wobbly
Room I stumble to my mother's door,
A shifting blur in the wall before me.
Her limbs are weak and rumpled on the sheet.
The empty braces glint. Their brightness hurts.
Pale pillow, damp hair, my father's shadow
Straining over her, sweat at his armpits,
Straightening, bending, straightening her leg.
Like knives her shrill cries peel the heavy air,
But he keeps at it, forcing tears back till
His eyes ache. The veins map out his anguish.
His false teeth tighten on that work of love.

## Singing Hymns Late at Night for My Father

While our mother, your dark-haired lover,
Lay paralyzed with polio,
We heard your crackling voice recover

A lost tune on the radio.
Never a singer, you nearly sang in time
"You Are My Sunshine," one more blow

Struck gladly for the March of Dimes.
Sister and I called up and pledged
Five bucks to hear it five more times.

For though on Sunday mornings you edged
Back from the pulpit microphone,
At home you offered like a cage

Of swallows your hopeless monotone.
By the old piano out of key
You sang too early, stopped too soon.

Last time I saw you, you had only
A seamy lyric in your ear,
Dandling the baby on your knee

To words you never let us hear.
If now, far from you in the close
Of night, we falter out of fear

Or out of tune or out of too much whiskey,
Bear with us, even in distress,
And when we raise the raucous noise

Of "Come Thou Fount of Every Blessing"
We will make an everlasting
Music with something missing.

# My Daughter Cries Out in Her Sleep

Before your small cries rescued me from darkness,
I had a dream of standing lamps and tables,
Of televisions staring into walls,
Of silent phone booths waiting on the corners
Of the world. Not a human soul in sight,
Much less a dark and furry animal,
A sniffing dog or a cat with eyes like ice.
Your sleep's alive; it moves on all fours
Like the bear forever shuffling through the zoo.
What innocent animal startled you from sleep?
Whatever it was, don't let it get away.
Keep with the animals. Love them fiercely
As they love and die. I had forgotten,
Before I sang above your trembling sleep,
How, like a leaping deer or a fox on fire,
Our lives come to us in a blinding dream.

# A Vacant Lot

One night where there is nothing now but air
I paused with one hand on the banister
And listened to a film aficionado's
Careless laughter sentence poetry to death.

It's twenty gone years and a few poems later,
The house demolished, the film man vanished,
The friend who introduced us to him dead.

I side with one old master who loves to tell
His film-buff friends that film is *like* an art form,
And yet my eyes keep panning the empty air
Above the rubble, as if, if I could run

The film back far enough, I might still start
For home down the darkened street from the newsstand
And turn a corner to the house still standing,

A faint light showing in an upstairs window.
Is someone reading late? Or is it the night
Our newborn lies burning up with fever,
And all the doctor can say is plunge her

In cold water, wrap her up and hold her,
Hold her, strip her down and plunge her in again
Until it breaks and she is weak but cooling?

Is it the night they call about my father
And I lay the mismatched funeral suit
In the back seat with the cigarettes and whiskey
And drive off knowing nothing but Death and South?

Somewhere a tree limb scrapes at a gutter.
The wind blows. Late trucks rattle the windows.
Never you mind, I say out loud to the girls

Away at school, There's nothing there to hurt you.
The sky is thickening over a vacant lot,
And when I leave there is a hard rain drumming
With the sound of someone up in the small hours,

Thirsty, his palm still warm from a sick child's
Forehead, running the spigot in the kitchen
Full force till the water's cold enough to drink.

# Locking Up

A shutter ticks or a finger snaps in my sleep
Or the silenced alarm clock clicks
As the long hand passes the hidden hour,
And over again he is locking me into his house,
Starting out of doors and bolting door after door
As he moves to the center of a nest of boxes.
First the lawn chairs drift off the lawn
To hunch in the damp garage under dust covers.
Beside them, the long black car is turning cold.
Now the door overhead starts to roll on its bearings,
Slithering over headlights
To ring into position on the concrete floor.
Now the gauzy wing of screen flaps shut,
The bolt of the inner door he slips into place
Is an oiled shell hissing into a rifle's chamber.
Now he is rattling the bones of windows, making sure,
Switching off the last light
With the pleasure of a safecracker listening for tumblers,
Laboring steadily up the stairs
To where a small eye burns against bad dreaming.
He is closing his own room now behind him,
Peeling his clothes off piece after piece,
Crawling into bed and drawing up the covers
Like a skin he can believe in.
Outside, he dreams, darkness is a slick black tarp
The gods pull over the earth and fasten down.

## On Hearing My Father's Voice
in a Dead Sleep

I know he must be breathing in
And out of somewhere.
Tonight he breathed my name
Into my sleep.
Tonight there are a few clouds
Left in the sky.
Just over the nearest mountain,
The two gray bells of his lungs are lit
And crawling with stars.

# Hybrid Magnolias in Late April

You bent to whisper to a small granddaughter,
Exposing the bald priestly back of your head,
Lifting her then and handing her to me:
      See you in April.

Never the same, these northern magnolias,
As the great starred candelabra ghosting,
Even before I left them, the deep-shaded
      Lawns of my boyhood.

And yet these too break wholly into blossom,
What somebody called the early petal-fall:
I walk out one day and the limbs are bare;
      Then they are burdened

With the flared tulip shapes of opening blooms.
Two rainy indoor days in a row, then out,
The sun is out, and a fallen constellation
      Litters the grasses.

What would you be up to this April morning?
Muttering to yourself, looking high and low
For the good stick fashioned out of laurel?
      I have it with me.

Patience. Lean back and light another Lucky.
Whatever will kill you dozes in your rib cage.
Read a few more pages in the *Little*
      *Flowers of St. Francis,*

Then throw a window open on the fragrance
Of even this, the northernmost magnolia.
By now the child you lifted in your arms has
      Slipped from their circle

To cherish and polish your crooked old stick
Into a poem of her own so tender and deft
I can hold its wrong end and reach you the worn
  Thumb of its handle.

## To Emily, Practicing the Clarinet

Early this morning, acres of birdsong
In the rising light. Now, as if still not
Dried out after dewfall, a quavering
Throaty note, and then another, from out
Beyond the hedgerow, or even across
The water, the cool reed-and-water strains
Of a young girl dreaming into the mouthpiece
Of a clarinet. Sometimes, my quick flame
Of a daughter, you lay down your instrument,
Are sassy, knowing, and brimful of banter,
But when those throaty notes rise from the earth
I hear you practicing as if your breath
Floating over that reed were innocent
Of the great empty air it has to enter.

## To Jennifer, Singing at the Piano

Here the silence, though peacefully broken
By birds or a fresh wind over the lake,
Can feel like a skein of loneliness shaken
Out over me musing into the late
Glow of a long evening, waiting for dark
To sleep. There the music, where you sit playing
And singing, thousands of miles south and westward,
Where the dark comes on in earlier evening,
There the music chastens the dark. You were
Always the quiet one, your hand at the nape
Of your neck for meaning, or your eyes that flare,
But now I hear you lightly singing, daughter,
As I slip gratefully off to sleep,
That tremulous "Bridge over Troubled Water."

# Reading the Mail in Early Fall

A small leafstorm of correspondences:

This gift book from a musical Welsh girl
Whose dark head launched a dozen seminars.
Somebody *else's* poems! and not the inward furl
Of lines by one more gloomy narcissistic sister,
But a woman's whole words for her dead and living men.
She writes her friend Tu Fu beyond the mountain
That she relishes the low-salt meat of monogamy,
Mild afternoons of wine in her own back yard,
Yet still she crosses herself and a continent
To come bedecked in clouds of scent and jewelry
To an old friend dying in a cancer ward,
Loved at long last by beautiful women.
He looks up lightheaded from his heaviest body,
Then shoves off eastward in the untied boat of Po Chu-I.

And this, what's this? A two-inch-tall giraffe,
All thanks to the slender elegant neck
And tilted head, the savvy contagious laugh
And the soft quick look away from heartbreak.
Little wooden long-neck nosing the leafless air,
Your frail crosshatch of stripes is scarcely visible
In the emptiness that shoulders your pure
Upward longing there on the polished table.
Brief shadowing shape of the coming loneliness,
Young woman who could wake up Robert Herrick,
What gives? I'll never know but luck would be my guess.
This creature's intricate as the strayed fawn at the salt lick
Or an Oriental silence, and nearly
Small enough to carry with me when I die.

I light the fire for tea, but it's not over.
Here's the mailman back with a packet he missed:
Leaf after glossy leaf, the face and figure
Of my daughter under the strange light of the East.
Here she is at her desk in the schoolhouse
Amid the upturned interrogative looks.
And here the question in her own lit face
Is not to be plumbed in the deepest of books.
In this one she and Kikko in Shizuoka
Are being Chubby Checker, hip to hip,
And here her gaze is blue and brimmed as the ocean.
I lift this smoky early-morning tea
To the brightness that falls from flowering young women,
For once spilling nothing between the cup and the lip.

## Blue Shades for a Daughter

Aprils ago we drank in your arrival
With the resined wine, the drifted apple orchard.
Kennedy was dead. We kept a stubborn vigil
For a war we dreamed our votes had thwarted.
You slept the hour away in a wicker basket.
These days you read the New York *Times* from soup to nuts.
If there's a shrewder question to ask, you ask it.
Evenings of wine, amid the clink of *buts*
And *maybes*, yours is the lonely, luminous *yes*.
You wouldn't miss a firefly in a holocaust.
This morning there's sunlight, the cardinal's treble
Saying who loses memory is lost.
The cool blue Japanese papers at the windows,
The skin-deep shades that lid our eyes are flammable.

## This Table

I see your grandfather through a haze of sawdust,
Though he seems under water, as if the eye somehow
Recalled the brackishness of nails held in the mouth.
He is making this table, his head bent when first
Sighted to the small plane beveling these edges
Smooth as the lip rim of a thin-blown wineglass,
Then, raised too quickly, knocking the lamp so it goes
Swinging its wafer of light across the darkness
Till it comes to rest in a shining pool the shape
Of this pine table, at which you now are toasted,
As, hidden by these draperies of blue and lace,
It carries the weight of a grandchild's wedding cake,
Which, as in the hillside miracle he trusted,
Seems to multiply, then melt in the mouths of the guests.

# Lecturing My Daughters

Listen a little. When my lone father
Called me down in love or hardly in anger,
I felt my own eyes shamefully flaring
        Under his mildness.

Sometimes he sang, and when he said scarcely
Anything but what he wanted me to hear,
I heard the sound of his own palm falling
        Asleep on my shoulder.

He took me walking in early morning,
In early evening, pausing in the lamplight.
Climbing a ladder, he let a swing down
        From a tree we lived by.

Last time but one I traveled home to him,
He took me walking just to show me where
A great tree hung its branches half a block
        No higher than a man.

Though there's not one tree where we are living
Strong or straight enough to hang a swing from,
With a little luck we will still do something
        Harmless together.

Little ones, I have raised the one father's voice
You know in anger. I will be quieter.
We will all walk quietly out together
        Under the lamplight,

And I will lower my own unsteady voice,
Hardly as musical as the one father's voice
I know, one rung at a time down the scarcely
        Audible ladder.

Maybe I am calling you home in time.
Given a little chance I had a father,
You are my children, walking in lamplight,
This is your childhood.

# A Small Rain

I sit with Mick McGinn and watch the swallows
Dipping till they nearly touch the roadway.
He tells me the rain is sure to return.
A heavy sky is holding the insects down.
At evening, off the road to Annaghmakerrig,
Two horses are running, their silk flanks shining,
The pool they run by starred with water lilies.
In the hayfield beyond them the sun goes down,
And a cloud the color of pearl is building
Over the simple hills of Monaghan.
Swallows are convening in the hollows
To keep me company for the final mile.
They swoop and twitter about a small rain
Coming, or somebody sure as the rain.

## To the Nuthatches

Stubby stoneware
Nestling, thumb of
Brightness, you were
Shaped under hands

Steady as rain
Over Cornwall
Where you came from
Cool to her hand.

You, memory's
Brave suddenness,
Flickering blue
Wings in the snow,

You quicken her
To vigilance
At the window
Of a stone wall

Windows ago.
Small as juncos,
Slate-blue, breasted
White underneath,

You are her birds:
Little one nudged
Into a stone,
Wingflasher blue

As memory,
And you, last one,
Unseen nuthatch
Lit with desire,

Downward climber
Headlong for dark
Earth, breast astir
With all you have

Left to tell her.

## Waiting for You with the Swallows

I was waiting for you
Where the four lanes wander
Into a city street,
Listening to the freight
Train's whistle and thunder
Come racketing through,

And I saw beyond black
Empty branches the light
Turn swiftly to a flurry
Of wingbeats in a hurry
For nowhere but the flight
From steeple-top and back

To steeple-top again.
I thought of how the quick
Hair shadows your lit face
Till laughter in your voice
Awoke and brought me back
And you stepped from the train.

I was waiting for you
Not a little too long
To learn what swallows said
Darkening overhead:
When we had time, we sang.
After we sang, we flew.

## Househusbandry

Early this morning when I idled around the house
Behind the carpenters, they were in rhythm,
As is only right, with the laws of square and shim
And shore-up, all oblivious of the hours
Of kneel and back-bend you had given to the borders,
The single peony that may or may not live
—No matter the ministry of sunlight and love—
The clematis still awaiting its climbing orders.

There was no question of a lack of water.
The poplars dripped. The carpenters mulled over tactics.
Would it be better to have had an attic
Or have strung up the former owner from a rafter?
Meanwhile the chickadees darted at the feeder
Through their mild but metronomic turbulence.
I went in for coffee and escape from consequence.
The carpenters discussed the cost of cedar.

Later in the fog I nearly sideswiped
A truck bound for the house with a load of siding.
No way he could have known where I was heading.
When I reached the parking lot the air was rain-swept
And the apparition waiting, hand on hip, was you.
I felt a sudden lightening back of my breastbone—
A plumb bob swinging to a standstill, gone
Featherweight on finding the hollow it was sounding true.

# The Visitor

Holding the arm of his helper, the blind
Piano tuner comes to our piano.
He hesitates at first, but once he finds
The keyboard, his hands glide over the slow
Keys, ringing changes finer than the eye
Can see. The dusty wires he touches, row
On row, quiver like bowstrings as he
Twists them one notch tighter. He runs his
Finger along a wire, touches the dry
Rust to his tongue, breaks into a pure bliss
And tells us, "One year more of damp weather
Would have done you in, but I've saved it this
Time. Would one of you play now, please? I hear
It better at a distance." My wife plays
"Stardust." The blind man stands and smiles in her
Direction, then disappears into the blaze
Of new October. Now the afternoon,
The long afternoon that blurs in a haze
Of music . . . Chopin nocturnes, "Clair de Lune,"
All the old familiar, unfamiliar
Music-lesson pieces, *Papa Haydn's*
*Dead and gone, gently down the stream* . . . Hours later,
After the latest car has doused its beams,
Has cooled down and stopped its ticking, I hear
Our cat, with the grace of animals free
To move in darkness, strike one key only,
And a single lucid drop of water stars my dream.

# Listening to Fats Waller in Late Light

*for Tom Molyneux, 1943–1977*


Once, in a Village bar, you kept us listening
To this music till we nearly missed our train,
Then hailed a taxi half-way to the station,
Your bright tie flying behind you like a little wake.
Now we are listening into late mountain light.

A little jazz in the South of France, Vence
Maybe, or some other town in the South
Of the heart, was what you dreamed you longed for.
Wine and daylight, the company of women
And children, the slow gold raveling of an afternoon.

The year we were for Italy, you were for France,
Their local wines so distant, yet the two countries
Closer in the end than our South and your North.
You were meant to visit us in Italy,
But your lame Peugeot would never make the hills.

Back home in the coldest winter yet, you nursed
Your broad-beamed Oldsmobile like a mother
With a sick child, bundling the engine at night
With old blankets, cajoling it to hold on.
Loaded with wine, it broke down on a Maryland road.

This is America. If this were in Europe
We'd send it to you on a sunny post card,
The lake water rubbing the stones with water-lights,
The small birches lonely even in their groves.
We came from your death to this beautiful place.

The sun goes down. He's doing "Honeysuckle Rose."
Were you speaking you would no doubt tell us
There is no clean way to come to this music
Save the one long mountain road of our grief.
There is no clean way to come to this place

Save the one long mountain road dead-ending
At the landing and nothing but the sunstruck lake.
This place appeals to your love of the sunlight
As our love for you appeals to the blue
Provençal light of your early absence.

For us the North Italian, for you the Provençal,
Those two skies nearer the one color than we thought.
Now the late light shines on our luck in each other,
A wish flashed over your shoulder as you left the party.
We are cooking the small-mouth bass and listening

To Waller, drinking the white wine of Verona
Since lately we get no kick from champagne.
Lucky the woman, lucky the man, relishing
Fresh dill, a little lemon and a little butter,
A little traveling music, a particular voice

Suddenly from no place at all in particular
Wishing us to live and be happy, have fun
Somehow tapdancing barefoot on the warm floor
Going cooler as the mountain sun goes down,
And the man himself, old friend, the man is doing

"Ain't Misbehavin'." We are getting mature.

# For a Suicide,
## a Little Early Morning Music

Most of the mornings here, when we awaken,
She and I can see what's left of the stars together,
And so we can this morning, even though lonely,

Imagining you. You were alight with elegance,
You were nervously and splendidly intelligent,
You loved the cities and you loved the shores,

You wanted to awaken with somebody.
Now, in this early morning, gathering
The last star's sunlight in a large warm bed,

We can see it clearly rising, rippling
A few temporary clouds with color
Over the water, and in the carved surf

A man of sixty, lean beneath his years,
Is swimming closely with a slender woman.
They must have awakened early together,

And then they thought of something they could do.
Sunlit in a place you loved, I can see you
Sunlit in another, you and I together

Down to our shirtsleeves in the brilliant streets,
Our neckties riffling as we round the corners
To Hester Street for veal and some wine from Verona,

Mulberry Street for pasta to carry home.
We were late for the train, and you were happy,
For you liked nothing better than wearing

A light suit, walking the streets in a hurry,
Packages under your arm for somebody lovely.
In Florence once, we saw the dark cool David

Of Verrocchio, and did not have the wit
To think of you running bareback through the summer.
From Rome we sent you a picture of Augustus

Looking under thirty in extreme old age,
But what we looked at longest was the beautiful
Bronze boy patiently and tenderly pulling

A thorn from his foot for several thousand years.

# Postscript to an Elegy

What I forgot to mention was the desultory
Unremarkable tremor of the phone ringing
Late in the day, to say you were stopping by,
The door slung open on your breezy arrival,
Muffled car horns jamming in the neighborhood,

Our talk of nothing particular, nothing of note,
The flare of laughter in a tilted wineglass.
Or we would be watching a tavern softball game
And you would come short-cutting by, your last hard mile

Dissolving in chatter and beer on the sidelines.
How did that Yankee third baseman put it, tossing
His empty glove in the air, his old friend
Sheared off halfway home in an air crash? "I thought
I'd be talking to him for the rest of my life."

Talk as I may of quickness and charm, easy laughter,
The forms of love, the sudden glint off silverware
At midnight will get in my eyes again,
And when it goes the air will be redolent still

With garlic, a high note from Armstrong, little shards
That will not gather into anything,
Those nearly invisible flecks of marble
Stinging the bare soles of the curious
Long after the statue is polished and crated away.

## Essay on Solitude

During his pain, Rilke dreamed solitude
An uncrumpled angel sleeping in the breast.
Forgive me, companion lying fast beside me
In the light, breathing morning, I tell you he dreamed wrong.

Human solitude is a slender single wing,
The only thing born whole, undamaged, lovely,
For all that flaring like a feathered wound.

Though we move in an appreciation
Of the sunlight, the sunlight will lengthen, stain,
And blind stagger out, saying its name was morning.
Think of all the heart-dark solitaries we have known:

Think of that dead cousin, lover of anything
That worked, who oiled his rifle till the bullet
Slept in the chamber, and then woke it up.

His curled hair kissed his ear like a feather.
Think of that live cousin, stunned by polio,
Father and mother wreckage in the small-town bars,
Whose ruined legs flop above the foot-rests of the wheelchair

He is dollying down the rampway to the school
Ballet. His face is rapt at the clumsiest
Of dancers, his gone legs wrapped in a rug.

Think of how it took our handsome old friend
All his life or merely one unbloodied hour
To slow his breath to sleep, emptying the doorway
That he leaned and laughed in. Think of the summer running,

His running with it, edging the shallow surf-foam,
  Arms swinging loosely, shoulderblades surfacing,
    Flashing at us briefly, one at a time.

    What can we turn to from that sunburst back?
  Sunlight through the empty doorway glitters on
The trefoil leaves of the green oxalis, the small
Wood sorrel I brought you on a whim a solid year

  Of our days ago, that still lives, that folds its leaves
    At the first sign of darkness, that opens them
      Secretly as eyelids at first dawning.

    We fall asleep dreaming of company.
  If we are not the perishing stars of flowers
That come and go in a little cloud of leaves,
At least we are the leaves themselves, folding, unfolding

Near our friends the others folded up forever.
  Each is one leaf hovering near another
    Dreaming two leaves can fly out of darkness.

    Leaves fall out of light. Each solitude owns
  A simple death shawl dreaming in some darkness
Its raveled hemline grazes the earth like a wing.
It hurts to think between us we have a pair of them.

## Autumn Elegy

If there's a figure for our time together,
Bright fall of days before you took your leave,
It is the old simple story of two roads.

Walking the creek below our empty houses
—Feeling the light divided by those leaves—
Brought me a figure for our time together.

One road slashes across the leaf-lit hillside.
The other rises meandering out of the south.
It is the old simple story of two roads.

The high road makes dry ground for the runner.
The walker in the low road carries a stick
Out looking for a figure for our time together.

Sometimes the one road falls to the narrow valley.
The other sometimes climbs away from the creek.
It is the old simple story of two roads.

There where they ravel together for a distance,
The runner may slow down to hail the walker.
This looks like a figure for our time together.
It is the old simple story of two roads.

## For My Cousin, Dead at Fifteen

Trying not to hear the static crackling
Through the music on the radio, I leaf
Through the dry photographs, passing the spring
Of Mama's polio, passing with grief
Paler than his skin my dead grandfather
In his swimming trunks, blinking in disbelief
At your best smile, your washed face shining over
The Boy Scout suit. Beyond the muddy creek
Behind you runs the railroad track, clover
In the field between, and kudzu thick
Enough for us to dive on, thick enough
For us in our war games to die on, stick
Guns lightly tossed before us as we slough
Off life after life. Hiding in hollows
Of the dense leaf-cave, we smoke Old Golds and cough
About our girls back in the States. But this
Is *my* yard. In your yard is the radio
Shack where you pass the rainy summer days
Cleaning your rifle. You make the stock glow
With polishing, cock your curious eye
Down the barrel . . . From the shattered window
Wire antennas climb the highest tree
In sight. I see you calling on clear nights
From Carolina to the windy . . .
Losing the signal as the static spits
And rattles the speaker, I switch it off
And rummage in the desk for a snakebite kit,
Broken compass, rusty hunting knife
Without a sheath. Rubbing my finger
Over the ring you carved for a neckerchief
Slide, I find not a raw spot, not a splinter.

# Chekhov: A Life

Hacking away at the Moscow newspapers,
Sweetening his arsenic stories
With a paste of charm, balancing the weight
Of a house of women on his shoulders,
Witty nursemaid and father to them all,
Shunting back and forth for hours every day
To nurse the dying Nikolai to death
Like some ghost of Dr. Keats, his own lungs fouling . . .
Then, in the interim at Melikhovo,
Doctor to bridges, to schools, to peasants,
To everything but his own rotting lungs.
"I'm terrified when I'm alone, alone
As in a frail boat on a great ocean."
But this also: "Probably the fallen
Angel betrayed God out of longing
For solitude, which angels do not know."
To Moscow and Olga, answering
His old notion of a wife, appearing
In his rooms and dancing like a drunken moon.
To Yalta, to Moscow, again to Yalta . . .
"As for the shortness of breath,
There is only one solution—not to move."
To Masha, at the end: "I kiss your hand."
To Olga and the doctor he was rasping:
"It is some time since I have drunk champagne."
With that, as if someone had asked him for it,
He coughed up his breath in a German spa.

## Robert Frost to Ezra Pound's Daughter from His Deathbed

Love is all. I tremble with it.
Romantic love as in stones and poems.
I'd like to see Ezra again.

Did I say stones? My mind said stories
And my tremulous tongue said stones.
Love is all I tremble with. It

Goes without saying I am gone.
Before I go for good I'll say
I'd like to see Ezra. Again

The years, the years rattle my spine.
How often must I not know what
Love is? All I tremble with, it

Rummages these old bones, scattering
Breath like the silvered leaves of birches
I'd like to see. Ezra? Again

His crazed head haunts me like a cloud.
All the dark certainties tell me
Love is all. I tremble with it.
I'd like to see Ezra again.

## Late December

While it's true that some conspiracy of stars
Persuades the eye the lumbering clouds are green,
That's beyond the pane, in the outer darkness.
Here the only green thing going is the spindly
Spiderplant at the window, and it looks cold.

Or look again: Is there a caught breath of green
In the curtain we may have just seen stirring?
It's not breath enough to quicken an ember.
The room is entirely lit by ice or snow,
Whatever sends that blue glaze through the window,

Furrows of snow or else the scraped sheen of ice
On a pond abandoned even by shadows.
The fire's gone cold that was in another room.
The man who sat here while it died was reading,
*Lear* it could have been, and he wanted weather

In view when he lifted his eyes from the page.
Now the shrill metal chair, brought in from the lawn
At summer's end, is empty, an odd blanket
Lapped over it like a mantle of snow
Or the folds of his last thought as he sat here:

In order to make believable Lear's cry
When he draped the cold Cordelia in his arms,
One consummate player sealed his civil tongue
To a scrap of dry ice, then emptied his throat
Of the sound the tearing away brought out of it.

# A Change in the Weather

Last midnight I walked in the hawthorn lane,
Hearing no sound, the scrap of moon so vivid
The night sky shone transparent as the day.
Suddenly I trembled at the slow lucid
Unfolding days I had such longing for.
What if the sky forgets to change, dawns clear
And clear till there is neither time nor weather?
How could you fly to me through changeless air?
Toward morning, the moon burned orange, then cloud
On cloud passed over till it was darkened,
And now this morning rain. Surely if so soft
A rain can out of nowhere cloud the broken
Moon while I am sleeping, so you can softly
Come and brush my waking eyelids with your mouth.

## Lament

> What I regret is many things
> in my future.
> —Melina Mercouri

One sore thing is the way
Our only friends will die
With nothing more to say
Than a long goodbye

Or no goodbye at all.
Another thing's the work
Shutting down to a small
Eye batting in the dark.

Then come the gay daughters
Gone from their wedding clothes.
Where you heard their laughter,
Hang a drained garden hose.

Write down dry veins, the hug
Of pain in every kiss.
Soon any catalogue
Of woe must come to this:

My body breaking down
Beside your body
Till one of us is gone
And the sheets are bloody,

And I am your lover
Taken by the darkness
Or a blank light forever
Where your lovely head was.

# Words to Accompany a Small Glass Swan

## 1

Cold midnight, Gogarty struggling in midriver,
Having slipped the Irregulars, leaving
An aftertaste of wit and his great fur coat.
He shook himself loose from its sleeves and was off,
Promising, stroke after stroke, if he got clear
He'd give a pair of swans to the Liffey.
Today, slipping indoors out of nothing worse
Than Dublin rainfall in a minor key,
I thought of Gogarty's lost coat, the warmth
He relinquished to plunge in the freezing river,
I thought of oceanic distances,
Shelter from storm, the home fire of your face,
Then found this small clear swan along the Liffey,
And a big *duvet* as soft as Gogarty's coat.

2

*Duvet*, it turns out, is merely the word for down.
Not downward down but airy upward swansdown.
That last Dublin morning rose clear and cool,
Though the sky was cumulus by afternoon,
Cloud drifts more friendly than unbroken light.
Breakable swan in my pocket, I walked
Those streets where shadows came and went like water,
And then, toward evening, bent to touch a lamp's
Furled shadow, and my fingers came away wet.
The clearest glass is misted by our breathing.
Think of the way translucent loneliness
Can augur a rush of love, and you won't wonder
When this brittle, sway-necked clarity gives rise
To warmth falling on you in a cloud of down.

# Working the Rain Shift at Flanagan's

*for Ben Kiely*

When Dublin is a mist the quays are lost
To the river, even you could be lost,
A boy from Omagh after forty years
Sounding the Liberties dim as I was
When that grave policeman touching my elbow

Headed me toward this salutary glass.
The town is grim all right, but these premises
Have all the air of a blessed corner
West of the westernmost pub in Galway,
Where whatever the light tries daily to say

The faces argue with, believing rain.
Outside an acceptable rain is falling
Easy as you predicted it would fall,
Though all your Dublin savvy could not gauge
The moment the rain shift would begin to sing.

They are hoisting barrels out of the cellar
And clanging them into an open van,
Gamely ignoring as if no matter
Whatever is falling on their coats and caps,
Though the fat one singing tenor has shrugged

Almost invisibly and hailed his fellow
Underground: "A shower of rain up here,"
He says with the rain, "It'll bring up the grass."
Then, befriending a moan from the darkness,
"Easy there now, lie back down, why won't you,"

As if the man were stirring in his grave
And needed a word to level him again.
His baffled answer rising to the rainfall
Could have been laughter or tears or maybe
Some musical lie he was telling the rain.

This is a far corner from your beat these days,
But why not walk on over anyway
And settle in with me to watch the rain.
You can tell me a story if you feel
Like it, and then you can tell me another.

The rain in the door will fall so softly
It might be rising for all we can know
Where we sit inscribing its vague margin
With words, oddly at ease with our shadows
As if we had died and gone to Dublin.

# Veterans

Backs to the window of the bar in Donnybrook,
Two bent but elegant soldiers remember
The Somme, living through it, how the river looked
Recalling the Liffey, the chilling number
Of wild Irish boys among the casualties.
The younger one lost an arm for his trouble;
The older, ninety-eight, first of the British
Officers to cross the Hindenburg, though able
To return intact, grows deaf to civil noise,
Yet quickens to the mention of a close
Compatriot bemedaled at the Parliament
Of London, who cheered all Dublin with his riposte:
"Insult the King and Queen? Not a bit of it boys,
Just couldn't take my eyes off the Duchess of Kent."

# With Thanks for a Shard from Sandycove

*for Seamus Heaney*

Late afternoon we idled on a bench
In memory of the man from Inniskeen,
The slow green water fluent beside us,

High clouds figured among leaves on the surface.
Then down along the strand to Sandycove
And the late-lit water, the sun emigrating

After a parting glance, the distant ferry
Disappearing soundlessly toward Holyhead.
We were laughing, riding the crest of company,

Your beautiful laughing wife and you and I,
When suddenly you tired of hammering
With a pebble at a stubborn boulder

And lifted it and dropped it on another
And handed me the chip that broke away.
I thought of the brute possibilities

In those farmer's hands, the place they came from,
What they might have done instead of simply
Dropping one stone on another to give

This pilgrim a shard of where he'd been.
You lifted that heaviness handily,
Keeping it briefly elevated in the air

As if more nearly the weight of a bowl
Of sacramental lather than the capstone
Of a dolmen in some field near Ballyvaughan.

Guilty as charged with a faithless penchant
For the elegiac, shy of the quick-drawn line
In the schoolyard dust, we prayed for nothing

Less than calm in the predawn hours and the laughter
Of disarming women when the hangman comes.
The sea grew dark, and then the dark was general

Over the suburbs, the window where I slept
Thrown open on the moon picking out the angle
Of a spade left leaning in a kitchen garden,

Shining like something prized from underground.

# The Enniskillen Bombing

*Remembrance Day, 1987*

"Showery with bright periods," said the forecast,
The way it does so many days in Ireland,
And indeed the arrowy soft rain fell

And the clouds parted more often than not
Above that watery parish, and the farmer
Walked in collarless from Derrygore,

The butcher left his awning snug against the lintel,
Two boys forgot their caps on the orchard wall.
Nobody looking at the sky or listening

To the weather would ever have predicted
That thunder would erupt before the lightning,
Blow the whole end gable of St. Michael's out

And bring the roof spars raining piecemeal down—
Not the slow-tempered grocer gone open-mouthed
With or without a cry as the windows roared,

Not the stooped pharmacist red-faced with grief,
Not the veteran of two World Wars in all
His ribbons, scrabbling with his raw bare hands

Through the choking dust for anybody's heartbeat,
Not the father wandering almost blindly,
Eyebrows seared from his face, who found his son

Still breathing only to knock the tip of his stick
Against his daughter's wedding ring, her splintered
Hand upturned in the rubble incarnadine

As the fuchsia banking a rain-swept roadside.

## Before It Happened

One afternoon a friend from the Falls and I
Drove out from Sligo into Enniskillen
For a quiet drink among old lamps and mirrors,

The glancing talk conspiratorial
As wives at the half-doors, silences freighted,
Lamplight pooled with sunlight on the polished bar,

The street outside a cleared-out Control Zone.
Across the street and up the narrow stair,
In a room with spring light swimming in the windows,

Fine as lace and firm as Blake's engravings,
The paintings of a dozen Irish wildflowers,
One after one, hung cleanly on the wall.

My friend the country walker, botanizer
Reared in the gutted streets of West Belfast,
Called every one by name from memory.

Bogbean, pipewort, grass of Parnassus,
Harebell looking so fragile it might tatter
In a breeze, yet stubborn as the stone ones

High on the capitals at Corcomroe.
We came downstairs into the slant of evening
And drove away in the unmolesting dark.

As we left behind the small lights of the town,
The voice at the wheel was naming constellations,
Orion, Cassiopeia, where they wavered

At first, then spread their nets of stars in the night wind.

# American Elegy

Let us acknowledge first our ignorance,
The sweet impossibility of knowing
What it was like. All of us, it is true,
Have been under water, but we were diving

Then for pleasure, and the water's surface
Was a skin of bubbles we could break for air.
Hardly one of us has sucked on airless space.
We have known fire, but very few have felt

The acid fog of smoke invade our sleep,
Ballooning the lungs of a dream until
We wake and smash the glass out of a window
And leap below to watch the rafters fall.

We have known hot light, but even the sun
On the blistering desert sets, and we
Fall asleep, if not under trees, in welcome
Oases of darkness. Knowing such fears,

We know nothing. We see from where we are
The blackened cockpit, the intricate thatch
Of wires, the tangled mess of tubes like entrails
Of the living. Our televisions catch

The bugle's thinning echoes at West Point,
The shadow of the lame formation booming
Over Arlington, and we are ignorant.
Feeling the abstract grief that swells our hearts

With blood like directionless water, we must
Imagine the usual fiery vision:
Virgil Grissom, Roger Chaffee, Edward White,
Breathing their deaths in that unquenchable light.

# Sleeping Out with My Father

Sweet smell of earth and easy rain on
Canvas, small breath fogging up the lantern
Glass, and sleep sifting my bones, drifting me
Far from hide-and-seek in tangled hedges,
The chicken dinner with its hills of rice
And gravy and its endless prayers for peace,
Old ladies high above me creaking in the choir loft,
And then the dream of bombs breaks up my sleep,
The long planes screaming down the midnight
Till the whistles peel my skin back, the bombs
Shake up the night in a sea of lightning
And stench and spitting shrapnel and children
Broken in the grass, and I am running
Running with my father through the hedges
Down the flaming streets to fields of darkness,
To sleep in sweat and wake to news of war.

# *R e e d s*

We are beginning one more time this evening,
Leaving our daughters and letting our lives
Uneasily down the hillside, leaning

Northward, where the moon means nothing to the heaves
Of stone that lie there starlit when the moon is gone.
One more time this evening the river leaves

The town alone to darkness watering the stones
Of faces down by the old poet's stinking riverbank.
In a little church whose walls fall sheer down

Into the riverbed, a couple of blank
Young thugs in leather jackets and their handsome man
In a midnight suit are laughing and clanking

Around in the parts of an ancient organ.
What do they know, we turn and ask each other.
When we turn back the one in midnight has begun

To touch a Bach Toccata like a lover.
One thug is gone, the other turns the pages
And eyes his dark companion, like a brother

Who lies back quietly in the dim-lit passages,
Then lends his hand with an assassin's skill.
In organ-light our vision of him ages;

We are shocked that he is nothing but a child.
With a little rotten luck, he could have gone all
Bloody piecemeal in Milano, killed,

Harsh headlights whipping the bloodlit wall.
Born in another country, he could be lying
Face up under water with only a reed to tell

The air his fatherland where his life is hiding.
Turning those pages, he is nothing but a boy,
Yet he knows well enough the skills of dying

To spend his evenings with a genius of joy.
Love, if we have listened, we will wander
Uphill to our daughters' eyes closed by the oil

Of youth and gladness, stare at them and wonder
As we lay a blessing on their breathing
Before we lay one other on each other.

This evening one more time it may be easy,
But it may not be, if we remember
All the trouble it took that organ wheezing

Before its small pipes rose into the reeds they are
And uttered a long low rustle from their nest
Down by that lonesome poet's stinking river,

Following an old inflection so a tossed
And driven man might find a breathing place.
Bright stars hollow the moon-bone, your loveliness

Hollowing the mouth-piece of my face.

## Basil

There in Fiesole it was always fresh
In the laneway where the spry grandfather
Tipped you his smile in the earliest wash
Of sunlight, piling strawberries high and higher
In a fragile pyramid of edible air.
Light down the years, the same sun rinses your dark
Hair over and over with brightness where
You kneel to stir the earth among thyme and chard,
Rosemary and the gathering of mints,
The rough leaf picked for tea this summer noon,
The smooth one saved for *pesto* in the winter,
For the cold will come, though you turn to me soon,
Your eyes going serious green from hazel,
Your quick hand on my face the scent of basil.

# Aubade to the Governor

> A statute of medieval Florence
> forbade lovers to make dawn
> serenades under pain of a fine or
> forfeiture of the lute, viol, or
> other offending instrument.


Dear Death, it is nearly dawn nine hundred
Feet or years above your fearful city,
And I am lying with her full of dread
I'll start to sing, for which you have no pity.
Forgive me, will you, if I hum a little
Under my breath, I am so criminally glad
To wake up prickly as a blooming nettle
Beside this rose of sleep in her own bed.
Besides, high up as we are, the sun itself
Cracks down on darkness with an early stealth,
And I start humming, I can't help myself,
So if by chance she should awaken, Death,
I pray you take it for an accident
And let me off, with my offending instrument.

# Words to Accompany
## a Leaf from Sirmione

You were walking alone
Down the slender almost-
Island of Catullus,
Walking the one green lane

Toward Desenzano,
In your arms the warm bread,
Olives, and the cool heady
Wine of Bardolino.

You were troubling your calm
Head for the local name
Of whatever leaves came
Springing fragrant as balm

To burden your pathway.
You broke a sprig off, touched
Your face to it, then placed
It in your hair, the bay

Of Sirmione, laurel
You tossed me in our room,
Wondering what its name
Was in your casual

Headlong lovely hurry
To sunbathe by the spindly
Willow rippling the friendly
Sunlit water where we

Swam and lazed and forgot
The laurel in the taste
Of bread and olives, the last
Wine fragrant as our thought.

Not knowing I was only
Awaiting all my life,
You gave your one bay leaf
Away in Sirmione.

I hid it in my shade,
That slender book where late
This gesture of leaf-light
Touches your shoulder blade.

## Soaping Down for Saint Francis of Assisi: The Canticle of Sister Soap

It took in, that human, that divine
embrace, everything but soap.
—Henry James


Winter sunlight in Assisi, and the birds tilting
        Their small wings over the roof-tiles,
And the mirror lilting from the bedroom wall,
        And the good and lovely and leering Signora
Giving us breakfast and a shower all to ourselves.
        There is soap in Firenze, there is soap in Bologna,
But more than ever there is soap this morning in Assisi.
        Henry, if you were here, we would soap your longest
            sentence down.
As it is we gather into soap whatever sunlight lifts in our direction,
        Shoulders, slippery breasts, long tapering backs,
Eyes clouded after a while against the burning,
        We are soaped all over, we are slithering somewhere,
We are two well-leavened loaves of fresh Italian bread,
        We are the morning hillsides of Assisi.
Great white doves of soapsuds fly from our shoulders,
        Great wings of dazzling soapsuds are waking
And flying and perishing into Assisi sunlight,
        And we are giving the beautiful dirt-loving Francis
More soap than even Henry James could ever think he wanted,
        And the good dead Francis is coming piercingly clean for
            once
Where we give each other love we never bought or paid for
        In this room of the profane and holy bargain.

## The Goods She Can Carry: Canticle of Her Basket Made of Reeds

Beginning I will praise a fine beginning,
  How the cloud of sun came up over the marshland
Where the reeds were green and supple and wind-bent,
  Not yet bent by the veiny hands of the craftsman
Who wove them in her basket while she watched and smiled.
  Even the first time, coming home from the craftsman,
She brought me a round and steaming loaf of bread.
  That loaf broken open on the kitchen table
Left loaves of sunlight piling in the empty basket.
  One morning a week the blouses and the bedsheets,
The schoolgirl smocks and all the delicate underwear
  She carries in the basket to the small Signora
And comes back grinning with an apple in each bare hand.
  On an ordinary evening, maybe an evening
Enough like this one it could happen even now,
  She comes with her basket of reeds overflowing
With basil and fennel, with sweet ham from Parma,
  With fruits of the commune, with flowered zucchini,
With a slender green bottle of Veronese wine.
  If I see her through the window I'll just
Whistle softly so she'll look up and right now she
  Looks up and sees me and carries her goods up the stairs,
Calling "Buona sera" to the neighbors as she climbs.
  Beautiful she brings the basket through the doorway
And pray do put it down I hear myself praying
  And let it sit there while the evening sky turns starry.
In the evening, in the late weather of October,
  The wine will cool on its own for a solid hour.
She slips her coat off as she turns to greet me.
  Ending I praise her for putting the basket down.

## Cold Water Dawn at Mountainy Pond: The Canticle of Italian Coffee

Friends, there are no Italian cities in this poem.
    There are the mountains and the lake of mountain water,
There are the scattered groves of birches and the lakeside stones,
    There is this girl whose breasts will go to Italy when she dies.
She is sleeping off another courteous awakening
    By these hands laid quietly on her till she rose.
She is sleeping and I am making Medaglia d'Oro
    With these hands that roused her to the ancient courtesies.
I am standing here in love in nothing but sunlight
    In this room not more than fifty feet from where she lies.
God love you, Wallace Stevens, whatever it was you said
    About the blackbird, I can tell you innuendo
Is less than inflection, my standing here making in love
    This coffee less than lying where she beautifully lies.
It is good nonetheless, this black cup of innuendo,
    Even if it's not her own quick blackbird fluttering
And whistling with me at the scandalous break of dawn.
    Why, when I lifted the coffee pot down from its cupboard
Its tin innards rang like the little bells at San Francesco
    Or those pulleys faintly knocking where the sailboat lies.
Remember, there are no Italian cities in this poem.
    There is this lovely sleeping, there is this coffee cooling,
There are these mountains and this lake of mountain water,
    There is my body in nothing but this mountain sunlight
That though it has much lovelier things to light
    Is lighting the pathway down to the morning water
Where in a second I will be diving cold and swimming,
    The only body swimming in this water's body
Stretching its blue and sunlit skin between the mountains,
    And I believe my love has given me strength to say
A prayer to the saints of sunlight, coffee, and cold water:
    May this beautiful place be more itself than Italy.

# With Our Wives in Late October

*for James Wright*

Wandering with weather down the long hillside,
We come to the slender reeds in the water,
All of us who lazed by our own rivers
       Summer and autumn,

Looking for redwings or leaves that were falling,
Light that was flying, the red wing of summer,
Never dreaming to be by one sure river
       Gathered together.

Now by the slender reeds in the water
Annie and Kay are looking for spiders,
Their own thoughts slender as the thoughts of spiders
       Looking for women.

Diligent spiders are our kindred creatures,
Friends of the season, and they are raveling
Somewhere lonelier than I can follow
       With all my singing,

But here's one Annie has suddenly sighted
Loitering brightly over the water,
Letting his legged and delicate star-body
       Flash us a signal

Clearer than water or the redwing's shoulder:
Some stars in heaven already dying
Light up the moonless night that is coming,
       Some stars are other

Bodies altogether, reluctant to say
How they become the light of October,
This spider, these leaves, these loveliest
       Faces of women.

## Lost Letter to James Wright, with Thanks for a Map of Fano

Breathing his last music, Mozart is supposed
To have said something heartbreaking which escapes me
For the quick moment of your bending to a dime

Blinking up from York Avenue, the last chill evening
I ever saw you, laughter rising with the steam
From your scarred throat, long-remembering laughter,

"Well, the old *eye* is still some good, anyway."
I thought of your silent master Samuel Johnson
Folding the fingers of drowsing vagrant children

Secret as wings over the coppers he left in their palms
Against the London cold and tomorrow's hunger.
You could not eat, I think you could scarcely swallow,

And yet that afternoon of your sleep and waking
To speak with us, you read me a fugitive passage
From a book beside your chair, something I lose all track of

Now, in this dim hour, about the late driftwood letters
Of writers and how little they finally matter.
You wrote to me last from Sirmione (of all things,

Sirmione had turned gray that morning), and it mattered.
We were together when the gray December dusk
Came down on snapshots of the view from Sirmione,

Sunlight ghosting your beard on the beach at Fano.
I had thought to write you a letter from Fano,
A letter which could have taken years to reach you

On the slow river ways of the Italian mails,
And now I write before we even come to leave.
We are going to Fano, where we may unfold this map

At a strange street corner under a window box
Of thyme gone to flower, and catch our breath remembering
Mozart breathing his last music, managing

Somehow to say in time, "And now I must go,
When I have only just learned to live quietly."
Last time I saw you, walking a little westward

From tugboats in the harbor, your voice was already breaking,
You were speaking quietly but the one plume of your breath
Was clouding and drifting west and away from Fano

Toward the river ferry taking sounding after sounding.

## *Sleeve*

As I lie and watch the angle of sunlight
Bringing its slow but true redemption to the screen

Of frost the night has left at my window,
There's nothing wrong with me except that nothing

I see awake is half so sharply focused
As the smallest eyemote, crumb of darkness in my dream:

A black rag flying from a house of cardboard,
Black hair on the shoulders of a man too tall

For the scrap of cover he'd pulled over him.
When I woke in the darkness of a room among rooms,

I felt this singular needling at my wrist,
As if a wind had unraveled my sleeve while I slept.

# Written in the Guest Book
## at Thoor Ballylee

This room needs furniture and the blue walls are cold.
Whether we should have been welcomed by the old ghost
We admire seems hardly civil to ask in County
Galway, where doors swing open to the rankest stranger
And they say whatever warms you when you are cold.
Still, this room needs furniture and the walls are cold
And colder in the resolute Atlantic wind.

This room needs music. I call old Tommy Nolan
Down from the streets of Galway with his great fiddle
And his frightening cough, to haul his chair up
Close to the measly fire we would be grateful for,
And lean into music. I call on Tony Small,
Laughing at the counter there in Cullen's, marvelous
Raw voice sweet with whiskey, to put down his glass and sing.

This room needs music and nobody here can sing.
Wind bangs the shutter. Long absences drum at the door.
Some voices we would gather the wind has scattered
All over this and other islands, some few as far
As the man who found and imagined this place, and then
Abandoned his soul to its battlements to die
In a French room without benefit of Galway.

We saw where they plowed him into that rainy churchyard.
He might have called his own bedroom the stranger's room.
Instead he chose this room where we stand wondering
How cold a man would call a room for guests the stranger's
Room, or how honest. Speech is exhaled into the cold,
Whatever we say, though rhetoric may turn to rain
And leave a lover's indiscretion in the air:

If you want to believe our life is possible, come
Look out the window where the wind blows a brief shower
Of leaves on the stream, swift with earlier rainfall,
And try to imagine that they love their vanishing
Merely to leave the surface untroubled and clear.
Then listen for breath in this room without music.
While you can hear it the stream makes a personal sound.

## For the Pause Before
## We Decorate the Tree


Dark pine tree hung with fragrance,
Your branches are all lit
With spiderwebs, small vagrants
Carrying light from twig

To twig, themselves the darkest
Stars I ever gazed on,
Vacant shinings like the points
Of some ghost constellation,

Its destinations darkened
But its ways still showing
Frail and luminous, broken
Light-net in the needles.

Dark pine tree light with spiders,
Stand there all afternoon
Lifting those fragrant branches
We will soon weigh down.

Dark pine tree beautifully
Dying into daylight,
Remind me late or early
How the evening gathers

Weight and gathers stillness
Till I lie down with her
And begin to touch her
In those places farther

From me sometimes than the stars
Are far from spiders
In your branches, than the years
Have fallen from her face.

I will kiss the good grave hollow
Between her breasts, her thin
Inner wrist, the cool shallow
Cup above her collar-bone,

All these and more, till near dawn
Light along her left wrist
Is a thread trembling from one place
Kissed to another kissed.

Dark pine tree hung with fragrance,
Are these scattered kisses
I imprint her with dark stars
Or simple darknesses?

## Trying to See Through
## Joe Heffernan's Glasses

These wiry gold frames that you gave me fit my head
As snugly as a skin, but the thick old lenses
Prove so strong I shut my eyes and the dark commences
To tell me where you are and what it was you said.

This long desk is a slab of walnut you might run
Your skillful thumb along to ascertain its timber
And maybe put yourself in mind of random lumber
In a pile that knocked your ear out when you were young.

The one ear you had left was good for fifty years
Before it sputtered like a candle while you sat in Mass,
Wondering if the good Lord God would have your carcass
Hauled out of Holy Redeemer before you lost your fears.

One cold Detroit December night before the snow
I blew in out of Marquette and a bad all-nighter
With your son my longtime friend and lovely listener
Who loves you like a patriot and calls you Joe,

Who lately takes a tone so nearly sure as yours
I have to perk up like a hound for fear of some live
Line that might have hidden in it somewhere how to live.
You gave us more than welcome and a little White Horse,

But hardly enough of freight trains and those brotherly men.
Locked out of hearing, you thought we didn't care to hear.
Nights now, you drive the city that you love and bear,
Taking a darkened turn away from home again

The way you hopped some darkened freight in the Depression,
Never caring if it went where you were headed.
You had a little money and you weren't downhearted,
And anyway all tracks would somewhere make connection.

If I open my eyes and take the dizzying risk
Of looking through your glasses, will I see the flames
Of my beloved faces gutter in their frames,
Or one more night train bound for any night but this?

Joe, it is almost baseball season in Detroit,
That murderous city where you live and make a living.
If luck holds out, the winds may prove forgiving,
Detroit may win the pennant and I'll see you in Detroit,

Or else we'll gather one day like lost settlers
By the roadbed, and hear the lone freight laying on its irons
The dead and living fathers' signal to their sons:
It's all right, boys, we can always grab a handful of rattlers.

# A Road Map for Reviewers

Dear enemies and friends, at last I have arrived
At the dead end prophesied and like it here.
Whoever dangled the open road before you
Was probably drunk or some kind of weirdo.
There is no such creature as the open road.
Most roads lead to Dallas or the Berlin Wall.
Rarely, usually less than once a lifetime,
Some bum strung out on redeye pauses to wrench
A roadsign in the blessed wrong direction
And you wind up out of gas and ambition
In a lonesome corner I won't breathe the name of.
The Italians say "Acqua in bocca"
For "Mum's the word." Nightly I test the local
Publican's brand on my Carthusian tongue.

# Two Anglo-Irish Sonnets

## My Mother's Lament for My English

"Don't ask me why, but more and more these days
The boy seems driven and bound for Ireland.
He's bought a cap, he's grown a beard, his hand
Forever restlessly polishes the glaze
On that walking cane. One night in a daze
He woke to a flashlight in his father's hand
Trembling the pages on the dictionary stand.
The word he was looking for stays and stays.

The boy finally told me in a grief:
Three in the morning, that brainy, wordy
Man had waked up tongue-tied by the Irish
Word *shillelagh*. Imagine my disbelief.
*Shillelagh*. All these years, and the English
Teachers still say his first love was Hardy."

## My Undersong

It's true. He stood there chattering in the buff
In bitter darkness, his nightshirt hanging
Where he left it when he heard you crying
To the empty pillow and tried to say love.
It had grown dark too early, and his bluff
But genuine tone had started you sighing
And after that the whole length of the evening
Argued the midnight would be raw and rough.

He missed his father. That day he had stirred
The early-fallen leaves and tried to wake him
With the very walking cane you mentioned.
He was a good man, however well-intentioned.
Come morning, muttering "The devil take them,"
He handed me the cane without a word.

# To the Swans of Loch Muiri

How she will love to see you here, you there,
Admiring yourself as if you were not
Simply one in a breathtaking hundred
Troubling this water to mirror your wings.
There is only the thinnest ridge of earth
Between you and that peerless shipwrecker,
Galway Bay, and yet you can coast serenely
As if you fell from the trees of autumn
To drift the surface of an inland pool.
You there, climbing thin air above the cloud
Of your reflection with a quick backward
Shudder and flourishing of your raised wings,
You are not the only beautiful one.
I am here to tell you just about now
There are great wings tilting in the airways
Over Jamaica Bay, outbound for Ireland.
Someone is leaning back becalmed as one of you.
She is flying in her sleep toward morning.
Now the earliest lamp of evening fills
A window set between us and the West.
The bluffs at my back have begun to darken.
One more midnight to live through, then to rise
Well before dawn and drive toward Kilcolgan
For the straight road south, the early morning
Dark a rush of roadside hedge at the window,
The right way dark as the bottom of some bay,
The only stars the lights of Galway City
And somewhere the vanished whites of your wings.
Keep them to my left and I will find her.
Right now our sky is turning toward that shade
I will wake in, a few of you are stirring
As if you had somewhere to go, singly
Or in the bowing couples beginning

To form and float together, and I feel
Already like that one of you I love most,
Wings whirring, long neck arched in expectation,
Half flying and half staying in the water.

## The Road to Ballyvaughan

The ferry shudders and scrapes against the stone quay
And we are moving, churning crosscurrent on the river
Nearly estuary, the gulls a billowy
Chaff of white above the whitecapped backwash, lovers
Young and old with their hair all windblown at the rails,
Histories little and long entwining their hands.

The ferry docks, we leave the river for the hills,
High miles of stony outcrop till the road descends.
Wildflowers we came for can wait until tomorrow.
This evening let's idle on the meadow grass, framed
On one side by limestone, by sea on the other side.
When the wine is gone, before we stir ourselves to go,
Let me raise between us a single fluted long-stemmed
Wineglass, empty of all but sunlight poured out on the tide.

# Talking Myself to Sleep in the Mountains

Longing, I have seen you in the water
Flare like a bluefish in your native place.
You are at sea level, dark-headed lover,
Twelve hundred miles of night southeast of here.
I have come up to thirteen hundred feet.
Hammer is with me, fly rod banging
On his shoulder as we clambered uphill
Sweaty with friendship, lying about the South.
We crossed the wind-burned ridgeback wild with berries,
Spooking and being rattled by a doe
In that dry cover, hiking up our packs
And skidding sideways to this run of water,
And the thick trunks smoking up the moon's half-light,
Tall poplar, beech—and saplings for the tent.
Now in the darkness we have pitched our camp.
Clear as it is, the creek will not pool deep
Enough to carry trout, so we fish out
Two cups of stone-cold water, bank the fire,
Bite down on that and whiskey on the tongue.
The fire is smokeless and the talk is good
And sifting into nothing like the fire.
The moon is blurred when I climb down to shiver
In the creek again and watch the light
Through stone-chinks stammer like a dream toward dawn.
Hammer is snoring when I climb back up.
This is a good place, it would be good
To sleep here with you and to bathe downstream
In the pool we are bound to find tomorrow.
It could happen. You could come here with me.
But I am laying on this going fire
The maps of every likely place I've been
For light enough to get back down to you.

# Impromptu Immersion in Tom's Run

Once somebody walked this Piney Mountain
Valley by the name of Tom. He must have known
This twisting run-off by its own right name,
Since afterward somebody named it for him.
I am up here following its silver
Whiplash for the first time. Hammer is good
Company, slow and garrulous as ever,
Stopping to fish in every pool of rain.
He fishes and I water down the drinks.
We slept last night inside the sound of water.
At dusk, the last light flashed from a wing-tip.
Now first sunlight stalks the creek-bed, warming
Us to hunger as we ramble downstream
Hunting for a trout pool. Nothing comes up,
Though Hammer says a trout could lie so still
In those cold shallows we would never see him.
Maybe so could I, I say, and strip down
Suddenly to nothing and am in it
Up to my knees, then flat-out on the stones,
Cunning and still as any mountain trout.
Climbing out I don't know what to call myself,
I feel so good in the growing sunlight.
I christen you nymph in the wood, says Hammer,
Who can't abide this craving after names.
If I caught a trout, he says, I'd call it trout.
Love, if I were with you by the ocean,
I'd lie down next to you and call it ocean.
Up here away from you, I can't let up.
What is the name of that strange white flower
On the forest floor? What is your own name?
I call that pool I bathed in Laurel Hole
For the one laurel over it, call myself
One solitude calling another home.

## Words Meant to Carry over Water

Believe me, daughter of those balmy waters,
I took my own bad time in getting here,
And it will take me more than a little
      While having my say.

One time a quick furlough in Massachusetts
Found me slow and lonely with my fast friends
Irish and Norwegian, gone on the grand
      Sibelius 2nd.

Iron was the element that hooked me up.
Everybody dancing, hallucination
On the pure blue smoke of the 1st violin,
      Up the spiral stair

And out the length of the horn's long rafter,
Swinging downward ripped my left thigh open
And my mortal buddies had to lift me
      Up to get me down.

Next year a sudden candle caught me by the shirt
And nearly burned my one good back away.
One enigmatic beauty whom I love
      Has made me warning.

If you travel north again avoid the water.
The only element you've left is water.
It hurts to call a mouth like hers a liar.
      She forgot the air.

The only thing I've done so far is listen
To my own story hobbling its way along.
Now at long last I can unbind my eyes,
      I can look at you

And my eyelids may not burn to nothing.
You are crossing the creek. You think the stone
Cold stones will knock the beauty from your bones
         But I know better.

I know you are coming to take my hand.
I know there is air above this water.
Here where these two cold currents run together
         There is scant sunlight,

Your bare back is stained with the leaves' own radiance,
Your wakening breasts are starred with darkness.
I know you are terrified of zero,
         Daughter of the south

Horizon, but you are coming anyway,
And suddenly I see my chances double
In this northern water, swimming for my life
         As I swim for yours.

## Watching You Sleep Under
## Monet's Water Lilies

Beloved, you are sleeping still,
Your light gown rumpled where it fell,

You are sleeping under the dark
Of a down comforter. The heart

Of dawn light blooming on the wall
Has not yet touched you where you still

Lie breathing, though it has wakened
The faint lilies, strewn and broken

Cloud-lights littering the water.
That you breathe is all that matters,

That you keep on breathing, lily,
While I wake to write this folly

Down, this breath of song that has your
Beauty lying among the pure

Lilies of the morning water,
Even though a light wind shatter

Them forever, and the too deep
Pool of desiring fill with sleep.

## Words to Accompany a Wildflower
## from Edward Thomas's Hillside

Listen close and delicate:
This wildflower is the late

Wayside violet that shines
Nearly hidden in the dense

Foliage where the hills of Steep
Gave the poet pause to breathe

On his way to where the war
Changed his name into a scar,

Knocked his fine heart from his chest,
Blanked the eyes that Helen kissed.

This wild blossom still has five
Leaves of starlight, tentative,

Dried in darkness for a year
Since I found it in the far

Hillside path where Edward climbed,
Holding Helen in his mind.

Now the nameless stars are out,
Now the name of Thomas floats

Like a star among the scars.
Here's his violet for years.

## A Screech Owl's Lament
## for Edward Thomas

Edward, the house is dark
As I begin to hear
What you bring back to me.
Though I am lonely now,
Nights had their loneliness
Before I found your name
In the lists of casualties.
Winter brought me a death
That shook my breath away
For a dear man lost
To anything I say
This side of silence.
Night on night the music
In me was an old hymn
Whose tune I could not carry.
Now though I am troubled
As the lost key rises
In a familiar air,
It would be worse to come
To an end of mourning.

Edward, the snow was deep
When you left for the war
And you and your Helen
Cooied to each other
Through the whitening fog
Till neither one could hear.
This evening in the dusk
Your voices came to me
In the gray dove's call
Beyond the tulip tree.
For a time that low song
Lasted, and when it died

It made a silence
Deep enough to breathe.

But now in the cold dawn
Comes a sound like the sound
You always listened for
Where you fell in the trenches,
A shivering whistle
Like a small horse whinnying
As he falls from the sky.
The screech owl in the woods
Has left his secret branch
And glided toward me.
Now he floats overhead
Like a ghost of the dark
And lowers to me
His wild descending cry.

# At the Graves in Memory

The land there rolls no more than the quiet river
Curves. Drifts of pine straw resin the ground.
Summer is remembered like a wild fever

That left the forehead when the sun went down.
That February day was mild as Easter.
There to the west of my abandoned town,

Shirt-sleeved gravediggers smoked at a corner
Of lawn unbroken by an upright stone.
Soft wind in the pines, the sound of water

Stilled in memory, the merciful brief drone
Of the old liturgy, and it was over.
My mother's body by my father's bones.

Winter. Easter weather. Long gone life-givers.
The land there rolls no more than the quiet river.

## Elegiac Anyway

It would be wrong to say that I am poor and lonely.
In nearly every way that matters I am getting fat.
The crabapple that will not bloom at least has leaves on it.
That young girl's breasts have made a small but firm down
    payment,
I have a fearsome death-defying lovely female wife
Of many years duration who when she's in a bad mood
Which is seldom can still say *Button your lip* with her lips.
And this is leaving altogether out that brace of daughters
Who'd make the seedy ghost of Lear anoint himself with laughs.
I have some visitors who leave me with a little wine.
But I knew a gentleman once said *Uncle* to his heart
Who scarcely took a drink or kept an evil thought for anybody,
And he's the one who won't come back to get his hat.

## Larkin

This first-name-only business beggars history,
As if the young mistook Ben Jonson's need
To keep a certain name immaculate
Till darkness tugged his wrist in the graveyard road.

Nearsighted and too far-off to wax familiar,
I would indulge the old formality
Of last names, since the man sank to his last hour
An ocean from my windows, low or high.

Larkin it is, then, with an added Philip
For those who would distinguish "English poet"
From, say, "hero of the Dublin shipyards."
His road was a hero's byway, but he knew it.

Larkin I have been reading now since sunrise,
Or rather, with the day thus clouded over,
Morning. His trains on sidings, his racehorses
Nuzzling the dusk, his taking the measure

Of rainfall while we still look for a cloud,
His chosen solitude, a singular light
Dispensed by water in a lifted tumbler,
A real day's shouldered and delivered freight.

"This is not the full portion of whiskey,"
I muttered, young and tanked on Dylan Thomas,
But now his angle's undeniable.
Somebody, somewhere, is breaking a promise.

Surefooting through the rain of rice and horn blare
Flattering some lovely daughter's wedding ride,
His tune is brassy, muted, grave, and just—
Jelly Roll's "Dead Man Blues" as the slow hearse glides.

Or think of it this way, as *L* for Larkin
Enters its cold-water flat in England's
Alphabet: Just now I was leaning forward,
His closed *High Windows* thin between my hands,

Palm to bare palm were it not for the poetry.
Knock in a nail and hang that image somewhere
Out of the way. Call it, should you think of it,
A man contemplating applause or prayer.

# Weather Report to My Father

You always took sharp pleasure in the weather,
Noting the angle of sunlight or saying
Merely to yourself as I am saying now,

Yesterday all day it failed to snow,
And now this morning fallen everywhere
The earth is six white inches nearer heaven.

I look beyond the vine-leaves at the window,
Beyond the tree-forks catching their wings of snow,
Beyond the acres of descending light

To a cold transparent Carolina day
For four years now accumulating nothing
But cloudless heaven breathless as the small boy

Waiting for you in the doorway all those
Winter evenings, who heard your only breath
Fall out of February like a snow.

## Miles from Newgrange
## at the Winter Solstice

The long-lit landscape of the summer solstice
Just over our heads, we stood in a seamless
Darkness. I touched your hand to the carved stone
Like some deep negative of Braille, each crevice

The whorl of a mind now wordless and flown.
Outside, the long shine on the river ran,
Shadows mingled, and a sudden fish leapt
And fell back scattering its reflection.

I heard the tenderness of your taken breath,
Felt for your hand again, and out we crept
Into the smell of mown hay and daylight,
Those stones left weighing the silence they kept.

Summer ended. Leaves fell. Now the window's white
With flurries or the full moonlight of late
December, we're too fleshed with desire to tell.
Beyond the waters, beyond the dark, light

Makes its once-a-year move down a channel
Intelligence left in the tumulus wall,
And while we lie together close as a fever
On childish limbs, it glosses for a still

Second a text as fine as a feather.
After long love, we should let dawn discover
The crevices between us, so we might not lie
Underground unread and dark forever.

# Wildflowers Left to Live on Knocknarea

After a night of rain like a waterfall,
The stony lane that winds up Knocknarea
Is a runnel of swift water winding downward.
You should wear your Wellingtons and carry a stick.
The stones are slippery and the dog at the gate
Is fierce and requires a cheerful word in passing.

The way up is steep and then steeper and turns
On itself to give you again and again
The whole blue bay where it rummages the valley.
Nearing the top, the lane is nothing but a gully
Of wildflowers where you stretch for every foothold.
When, having stopped for breath, you can lift your eyes,

That stone shape just beginning to clear the high
Horizon is a queen's grave or nothing but stones.
Just over the final ridge, you can see it whole
At last, tired out and your breath entirely vanished,
So you simply sprawl out headlong in the heather
In an attitude a stranger might take for prayer.

But you are alone on the windy mountaintop.
North of that lighthouse are Rosses Point and the cliffs
Of Donegal. South and wild are the Mayo mountains.
If only the mist would lift you could see five counties.
But the low sky returns you to the near at hand.
There, nesting in the heather, you may uncover

The delicate wild blue harebell of Knocknarea.
If I know you, you will want to look at it long
And dream you can breathe the air it breathes forever,
Which is only to dream you can hold your breath forever
And not give in to the slow intake and exhalation
That keep you moving, even if your only way

Is the watery lane back down the mountainside.
The wind swings northward and cold. The mist is lifting.
It is high time you were picking your way downward.
Look for the blossoming ditch that brought you there.
Look. There is the spring gentian, there the small wild thyme.
Your turn has come to leave them there for another.

# Swamp Mallows

Nearly still water winding among the grasses.
Low white clouds of blossoms, "useless for picking
Since they wilt within an hour." A cumulus sky.
This looks so much like a version of the calm
We might slip into out of troubled waters,

You will forgive me if I sense my father
Just out of sight around some mallowy bend.
At the painting's edges time unravels anyway,
So we might as well let it be summer,
Eastern Carolina, 1949,

The moment he leans down to steady the johnboat
Beside the dock for me to clamber into.
Then, when he has me balanced in the bow,
He reaches me the rods and tackle box
And steps down gingerly into the business end.

This time he has only a single paddle.
We won't be going far, and he loves the quiet
As the boat ripples into a channel
So narrow we can touch the brush on either side.
Then it is all drift and fish—the sun lowering,

The "weedless" hooked lines skimming the bottom for bream—
Casting and reeling till down the long perspective
Of the evening we grow weary of fishing
And catching nothing, lay the gear down carefully
In the slick boat-bottom and give in to drift.

My father's hat is tilted over his eyes
As we float in the freedom of saying nothing
Till warmth and water ferry us into a drowse.
Anybody watching from the bank would see us
Slide unknowingly under a little footbridge

Where a few old ones with kerchiefs on their heads
Are lifting their crab lines with the patience of heaven,
And then we scrape a tree stump and wake up to this:
Nearly still water winding among the grasses.
Low white clouds of blossoms. A cumulus sky.

We have come around in a backwater silence
Still white with mallows. In the face of all this air
And water and slow-to-perish brightness,
We might for once imagine death has been neglectful
And surrendered our passage to be banked with bloom.